WALKING BY FAITH

ON PURPOSE

A biblical perspective to law of attraction

By Lucindy L. Lumu

Father God,

I pray that each and every soul reading this book

will be blessed spiritually, physically, financially and

emotionally. I pray Father God that your Spirit will be made

manifest upon the reading of this book! Let every feeling,

thought, word and desire be purified and let your desires

Father God be our desires!

~Amen

Table of Contents

DEDICATION

To the most awesome and awwmazing gifts in my life: Brendon, Theresa, Tonni, Jonathan, Loren & Andrew; you're the reason I strive for greatness. You're my smile, my encouragement and my motivation! It is you guys that inspire and motivate me to be a better me! I thank God everyday for blessing me with each of you, because without you, I wouldn't be who I am today!

-Love Always, Mom

INTRODUCTION

Jesus told him, "I am the way, the truth, and the life. No one can
come to the Father except through me.
-John 14:6

If "truth" is the highest form of reality, then
according to John 14:6, God "IS" truth, thus being the
highest form of reality! Yet, the number of unbelievers is
staggering! I often times ask myself, how is it that those
who do not believe in the God of this universe, explain the
sunrise and sunset, conception and birth or even the single
seed that goes into the ground and yet miraculously yields a
multiplied harvest? Not sure? I'm going to do my best to
convince those who are on the fence, to get off the fence
and embrace a Savior, Redeemer, Provider or as I like to
call Him.... Friend!

Jesus is always waiting on us to receive His love. He's there to provide, not take away, to heal not make sick, deliver not to imprison, give life, not to kill! We have been brainwashed into thinking that we are powerless, and this couldn't be the farthest thing from the truth! Truth is...we are POWERFUL! When we were made in the image of God (Genesis 1:27), we were endowed with His power! Our heart, mind and mouth were created as a part of man's anatomy in order to be used to co-create with our Creator and heavenly Father.

Science teaches us that energy cannot be created nor destroyed! Quantum physics proves that everything is vibrating even you and me! This scientific fact proves that God *is* energy! God cannot be created nor destroyed. This is why He created us in His image where we share His *energy*. He spoke and invisible matter became solid matter. Our feelings, thoughts and words are vibrating consistently!

Feelings, thoughts and words are *energy* and are constantly changing the world around us, as we know it!

You see God cannot fulfill His will and plans unless He has a vessel to do it through. This is why He instructs us in His Word to guard our hearts (proverbs 4:23), and set our minds above (Colossians 3:2) because as a man THINKETH so is he (proverbs 23:7) and most importantly, to remember that LIFE & DEATH is in the POWER of the tongue (proverbs 18:21)! God formulated man to think and speak things into existence. Yet we've been programmed to "think" we must "work" hard and "toil" in order to succeed. Life was never created to be difficult for the children of God. We were never created to struggle. This kind of thinking displeases God (Hebrews 11:6). If you hold these wrong beliefs, I encourage you turn over a new leaf, a new way of thinking! I urge you to put down the struggle and pick up the POWER! It's within YOU!

God is waiting for your command and your faith! You will find that God is not only real, but the power that we inherited from our heavenly Father is also real. You will soon come to see as He is revealed in the pages of this book. So grab a snack and your favorite beverage and enjoy this read.

TRUTH

"The truth is like a lion, you don't have to defend it.
Let it loose. It will defend itself."
-St. Augustine

Truth is...we were given the power all along to conquer and achieve anything we put our minds to! Literally! Some like to believe that they are "waiting" on God, when truth is; God is really waiting on us!

All of us were given a purpose to fulfill in the earth. God knew our purpose before we were born ("before I formed you in the womb I knew you, before you were born I set you apart..."Jeremiah 1:5). Its up to us to "allow" God to perform His purpose for us.... through us! And in order to perform God's perfect will through us, we must be born again ("Truly, truly, I say to you, unless one is born again, he cannot see the Kingdom of God" (John 3:3). You see, though God has given us the power to achieve whatever we desire, He's given us a choice to use it for good or evil. It is up to us to accept God into our lives through accepting His

Son Jesus. God is very clear in how He feels about those who come into "stuff" apart from Him: "For what will it profit a man, if he gains the whole world, and loses his own soul..." (Mark 8:36). God knew the power He gave *man* to create whatever he desires, but with that power came *free will*/choice. God wants us to *choose* Him in order to carry out His purpose for our lives.

We were created to fulfill God's purpose for us in the earth and in order to fulfill it, we must become one with God. John 15:5 states that "I am the vine; you are the branches. If you remain in me and I in you, you will bear much fruit, apart from me you can do nothing." It's imperative that we have relationship with our Creator and heavenly Father.

We must also realize that we have an adversary that is warring for our soul as well. John 10:10 tells us that "The thief cometh not, but for to steal, and to kill, and to destroy....". Satan disguises himself as an angel of light and he imitates the "blessings" of God, but if you are walking in "truth", also referred to as "walking with God", then you will know that Proverbs 10:22 tells us "the blessing of the Lord, it maketh rich, and he addeth no sorrow with it." So understand that you can come into "stuff" apart from God, but be prepared to reap the sorrow that will be attached to it.

God's Word, the bible, also known as the "Truth", is the tool we are to use in order to conquer and accomplish "stuff" in our lives. Look at the Word of God like your secret weapon. Hebrews 4:12 tell us "For the Word of God is alive and active. Sharper than any double-edged sword, it penetrates even to dividing soul and spirit, joints and marrow; it judges the thoughts and attitudes of the heart". So you see, the Word of God is the source of our power! In this book we will look at how to line up our thoughts, words and emotions with the Word of God in order to erect our God given purpose and live an abundant life.

POWER OF THOUGHT

"Whether you think you can, or you think you can't...you're
right"
-Henry Ford

Everything in our physical world is made up of

vibrations of energy. Likewise with our thoughts, they too,

are made up of vibrational energy. Science explains that our

subconscious mind is what's communicating to our body in

order to make sure that the things we don't think

about...gets done. For example, we don't have to tell our

heart to beat, blood to flow or even to inhale and exhale.

These are automatic.

In order for the body to think a thing or do a thing

"automatically" it must be programmed in the subconscious

mind. The way to program the subconscious mind is

through repetition. It is said if we have a repeated

thought(s) we are creating an imprint of that thought into

our subconscious mind. We are creating a mindset,

behavior or attitude that will eventually become

"automatic", thus, we will "automatically" attract situations, people, circumstances that mirror our attitudes, behaviors and mindset. We won't have to toil for it! This is why Proverbs 23:7 tells us "For as he thinketh in his heart, so is he." We become what we think about.

Our minds are like gardens and our thoughts are the seeds. Whatever we take into our thoughts, through television, conversation and/or audio, we are planting seeds into our minds. Which is why its important for us to be cautious as to what we set our minds on. Philippians 4:8 instructs us to "Finally, brethren, whatsoever things are true, whatsoever things are honest, whatsoever things are just, whatsoever things are pure, whatsoever things are lovely, whatsoever things are of good report; if there be any virtue, and if there be any praise, think on these things."

Our thoughts produce "stuff". So what "stuff" are you accumulating into your life? If we learn to govern our thoughts, then we can control our outer world instead of allowing the outer world to control us. We are spiritual beings. As spiritual beings we were created to affect the outer world from the inside out, not to allow the outer world to affect us from the outside in! This mind power takes practice and must come from God. In 2 Corinthians 10:5 it states "Casting down imaginations, and every high thing that exalteth itself against the knowledge of God, and bringing into captivity every thought to the obedience of Christ." The more we refuse negative thoughts, the easier it will become to think positive. The more positive we are, the more we will begin to attract the "stuff" we actually want into our lives. On the flip side, the more negative we become and give our focus to that which we don't desire, the more we will continue to attract the "stuff" we don't want. This ladies and gentleman is what scientist like to refer to as *the law of attraction*! Law of attraction states that like attracts like be it good or bad. As believers, we call it sowing and reaping.

So be mindful of what you are giving thought to and then ask yourself, is this the harvest I want to produce in my life? Remember, according to Galatians 6:7 "Be not deceived, God is not mocked; for whatsoever a man soweth, that shall he also reap." So make sure you are sowing positive thoughts and deeds!

POWER OF WORDS

"Death and life are in the power of the tongue: and they that love it shall eat the fruit thereof" -Proverbs 18:21

Have you ever paid attention to the words you speak out of your mouth on a day-to-day basis? For example: "I'm broke", "I'm sick", "and I'm depressed", just to name a few. These are affirmations. Affirmations are words used to "affirm" or seal things in our lives. Unfortunately, most of us don't realize we're sealing or affirming such negativity, thus creating and repeating a negative filled life!

According to proverbs 18:21 death and life are in the power of the tongue, which means God created us with a power-filled weapon designed to either bring us blessings or curses. He left the choice up to us. This is why it's so important to be cautious as to what we allow to come out of our mouths. The only way to control that which comes from our mouths, is to yield ourselves to the Holy Spirit of God! James 3:8 states: "but the tongue can no man tame; it is an unruly evil and full of deadly poison". This is why people don't understand how "they" bring things upon themselves. Often times, we want to blame the devil or say God "allowed", when the truth is...WE brought negative circumstances, illness, lack, depression...on ourselves through our WORDS, allowing deadly poison to spring forth and affirm such negativity over our lives. People don't give thought to the power behind words, which is why they use them so recklessly. My desire is for you to look at your words like seeds. Just like our thoughts, our words are like seeds as well. Ready to yield a harvest the moment they are planted.

We must keep in mind, scientifically; everything is vibrating and giving off energy. Like thoughts, our words are also giving off energy and depending on which frequency we are tuned in to, this will determine what we will attract into our lives. Negative thoughts are said to vibrate at a low frequency. Positive thoughts are said to vibrate at a high frequency. So if you want to create a healing in your life, tune yourself into a positive frequency and keep your mind and words in a positive state. You feel, think, speak and see yourself healed.

According to Romans 4:17, we must ".... calleth those things which are not, as though they were." Keep in my mind, we BECOME what we think about, we CREATE what we speak about and we ATTRACT what we feel! We have been brainwashed to believe that we must SEE it in order to believe it, but I am here to tell you that's the furthest thing from the truth! God is calling us to BELIEVE it BEFORE we see it! This takes faith, which we will cover.

We were given DOMINION according to Genesis 1:26 ".... and let them have dominion over the fish of the sea, and over the fowl of the air, and over the cattle, and over all the earth, and over every creeping thing that creepeth upon the earth." Dominion is just another word for AUTHORITY!

So if God gave us authority, why are so many of us NOT walking in it? Why do we roll over and allow life to happen to us? I'll tell you why, its because we haven't been told that we are powerful! Some of us have been told, but lack the faith to believe it! Our authority is what gives us the right to command whatever we want into our lives! It's just like any person in a position of authority; they are given certain rights to make decisions that those who otherwise do not have authority couldn't make. Do you see how this language is all wrong? We were trained to believe that ONLY those in "authority" positions have the power. Again, this is the furthest thing from the truth. Don't get me wrong, certain jobs require persons of leadership in order to function and operate. However, what I am trying to get you to see is, even though there are people in positions of authority, we have the power to control our outcomes and destiny. Just because there are people over you, does not mean they control your destiny.

You were given dominion as well and if exercised correctly, no circumstance, situation, boss, judge or police can ever harm or bring any injustice upon you that you don't allow! What I am about to share with you next is going to be life changing! If you do this next thing you will erect the blessing of God in your life full throttle! Are you ready? I can sum it up in one word.... DECREE! A decree is an *official order* issued by a legal authority! There goes that word authority again. Job 22:28 states "Thou shalt also decree a thing, and it shall be established unto thee..." just like judges, we have the legal authority to give an official order and God promises that it will be established! Ladies and gentlemen.... it doesn't get any better than that. So I encourage you, whatever negative thing you have going on in your life, start decreeing what you want. Exercise your DOMINION/AUTHORITY and serve satan your OFFICIAL ORDERS! The situation will have no choice but to manifest!

FAITH

"Now faith is the substance of things hoped for, the evidence of things not seen" –Hebrews 11:1

Often times, churches will tell their congregation to "just have faith...". But if you were anything like me, you were left wondering...how do I do that? I always knew there was something more to this thing called faith. I wondered, if "faith" was so easy, why are we not seeing the greater works that Jesus spoke of over in the book of John? Why are we not witnessing this power being played out in our churches and lives? I never was okay with being an average, Sunday morning, career Christian. I wanted and desired more! It wasn't until 2015 God begin to put the pieces together for me. As He began to teach me, it all started making sense.

He explained to me that "faith" is equivalent to "emotions". Emotions are energy in motion. Where you tend to give your energy, the most, is where your faith is. I will cover this topic in greater depth in another chapter. Our heart tells us how to think and our thoughts tell us what we believe and if you look close enough at the sum total of your day- to- day thoughts, it will tell you what you believe. For example, if your thoughts are about not having enough, wishing you had more and telling yourself you need more money, this is your belief system and sense you believe in poverty and lack, your life will reflect that and you'll stay needing, wanting, wishing and never having enough. If you believe you're sick, your life will reflect that and you'll stay sick. But the opposite is also true, if you believe you are wealthy, you will find your life attracting wealth. If you believe you are healed and healthy, your life will reflect your healthy self.

What we have to understand is, from a scientific point of view, our bodies, thoughts and words are constantly giving off energy. Depending on our mood, it has been scientifically proven that those who are depressed, angry and stressed are vibrating at a low frequency. Those who are happy, carefree and positive, they are vibrating at a high frequency. It is for this reason, God instructs us through His Word over in Philippians 4:8 "Finally, bretheren, whatsoever things are true, whatsoever things are honest, whatsoever things are just, whatsoever things are pure, whatsoever things are lovely, whatsoever things are of good report, if there be any virtue, and if there be any praise think on these things."

God knows that by us thinking on these things, it will cause us to vibrate at a higher frequency, thus being able to attract that which we desire into our lives. On the flip side, He knew if we did not have our minds in a positive place we would ultimately attract that which we do not desire into our lives as well. This is also why in

Hebrews 11:1 it states that faith is the substance...that substance is that energy we give off, its invisible to the naked eye but very much so visible to those studying science and can witness under microscopes what happens to matter when we're being negative vs. when we're being positive.

Therefore, what we believe is constantly being attracted into our lives. Faith is never mentioned as to being positive or negative, which means we can have negative faith yielding negative results and circumstances. However, if we learn to direct our faith in a positive way, according to Mark 11:23 we can speak to the mountain and tell it to move and it will move!

When we line up our thoughts, words and emotions and carry them out with dominion, there is nothing we can't achieve! We were all given a measure of faith according to

Romans 12:3, its up to us how we use it! According to Matthew 9:29 that states "...according to your faith let it be done to you." If you're trying to manifest a six figure income, but your faith can't seem to get past your 30K dollar a year job, guess what, you're going to be stuck at the 30K level never seeing the 100K level made manifest in your life. So feel it, think it, believe it and speak it and then you will achieve it!

POWER OF EMOTION

"Keep thy heart with all diligence; for out of it are the issues of life." –Proverbs 4:23

Our emotions are the catalyst that create the things we either want or don't want. E-motion is just energy in motion! Every emotion is setting the course for what you are attracting into your life. Remember, like energy is going to attract like energy. So if you are in a negative mood, you are going to attract more situations, circumstances and/or people that will match your mood. This is why we are to be mindful of our attitudes towards others as well as towards our circumstances.

We are always in a state of reaping and sowing whether we acknowledge it or not. Just like thoughts and words, our emotions are also like seeds being sown into the atmosphere. If you don't want to reap a negative harvest of negative people, negative situations and/or negative circumstances, check your attitude and change it to a positive one. Governing our thoughts, words and emotions is like controlling a radio station, we control what station we want to listen to. So if something is being played out in your life that you are not feeling, or do not like, then change the station. Find a station or rather an attitude, thought and/or conversation that is going to reflect what you desire and where you desire to be! Stay focused and in tune with your vision and goals in life!

Being focused and staying focused requires emotional discipline. Staying in tuned to a negative emotion too long, will corrupt the manifestation process. You will begin to attract the opposite of what you desire and your negative emotion will begin shifting the things in your life in order to match the negative feelings you're giving energy to. This is why people say, don't give too much energy to that. Scientifically speaking, our emotional energy is what allows things to manifest quickly.

As a man or woman of God, we understand that God is love and operates out of a place of positivity. In order to manifest the desires that God created us to fulfill, we must become one with Him and allow His Holy Spirit to operate through us in love. This is also why it is important to be born again and accept Jesus into our lives, so that we are manifesting God's desires for our lives and not our own. (John 3:3 Jesus answered and said unto him, "Truly, truly, I say to you, unless one is born again he cannot see the Kingdom of God.") "For it is God who works in you, both to will and to work for his good pleasure" (Philippians 2:13) . There are plethoras of "spirits" that can operate in and through us, which is why we as believers need to be filled and led by the Holy Spirit. The fruit of the Holy Spirit is love, peace, patience, kindness, joy, goodness, self control, gentleness...according to Galatians 5:22-23. If your emotions are not reflective of such fruit, then its time to reassess and stop eating rotten fruit that is making you sick. Eat of the fruit of the Holy Spirit so that you can start manifesting its nutritional value! Always know that whatever you are feeling emotionally, you are attracting that current emotional state. So keep your emotions in check and in a positive place in order to yield positive results

EXPECTATION

"For I know the thoughts that I think toward you, saith the Lord, thoughts of peace, and not of evil, to give you an expected end."
–Jeremiah 29:11

Expectation is key to what you are believing God for. Expectation is the HOPE in Hebrews 11:1 that states, "Now faith is the substance of things hoped for, the evidence of things not seen." I guess you can read it as now faith is the substance of things expected, the evidence of things not seen. Whatever you expect out of life, that is what you will attract into your life. If you don't expect anything, you won't accomplish anything. Expectation is tied to our emotions. If we are emotionally in a good place, we will find that good things tend to play out in our lives. However, if we are emotionally in a bad place, it seems like everything about our day tends to go bad. I guess you could say, we expected it. Have you ever said, "what else can go wrong..." or "I know this is not going to be a good day...." These are all decrees of negative expectations. Remember, your emotions attract whatever energy you are giving off. Negative energy attracts negative energy. Positive energy attracts positive energy.

If you believe great things are in store for you, then great things will begin to line up in your life. If your attitude is of self-pity and undeserving, well, it doesn't take a rocket scientist to figure out what kind of life you will lead. Think about it; would you drive through a fast food restaurant and place an order, then drive off? Ridiculous! Right? This is how crazy it would be if you tell God to bless you with a promotion and then don't expect it. You must wait on the order to be fulfilled or made manifest in your life!

The only way to change your negative expectations into positive expectations is to learn what God has to say about whatever you desire. His Word is full of promises.

Find scriptures surrounding your issue and affirm them

daily. Eventually you will come to expect more out of life!

PROSPERITY

"Beloved, I wish above all things that thou mayest prosper and be in health, even as thy soul prospereth." – 3John 1:2

Lack is NOT of God! I understand that there are those who believe that the poorer you are the closer you are to God. This is a lie from the pit of hell! I urge you to stay away from such perverse mindsets. God's desire for us is to prosper in our finances, health and souls. There are societies, cultures and some churches that teaches that there is not enough and will use media propaganda and fear tactics to get you and I to believe that because the economy is "failing" we must also be failing or lacking. The devil is a liar! The economy failing has nothing to do with God's resources according to Matthew 6:26 "Behold the fowls of the air: for they sow not, neither do they reap, nor gather into barns; yet your heavenly Father feedeth them. Are ye not much better than they?" God is abundance! His name is Jehovah Jireh (God Provides).

Decree abundance in your life and it shall be given unto you. According to Psalms 34:10 "The young lions do lack, and suffer hunger: but they that seek the Lord, shall not want any good thing."

What we must keep in mind, in order to activate the blessings of God, doubt and fear must not be present. Fear is the opposite of faith. God said, "But without faith it is impossible to please him: for he that cometh to God must believe that He is, and that He is a rewarder of them that diligently seek Him." –Hebrews 11:6. We must train ourselves to line our thoughts, words and emotions up with the Word of God in order to see the blessings of God made manifest in our lives.

IMAGINATION

The greatest battle you will ever have to fight, will be the battle over your mind! Satan knows how powerful our minds are and therefore creates imaginations or thoughts in our minds that keeps us from succeeding in our health, finances, relationships and life. He knows that if he can keep us distracted with things that are going to sow seeds of depression, anger, lack and other negative vices, then we will never fulfill purpose! Our purpose is tied to our happiness, peace and passion! So we are instructed to cast down these negative imaginations, in other words, cancel them out and give them no life! It's important to find positive things to fill your mind with. Occupy your mind with your purpose and/or vision. Use your imagination to visualize yourself as the person you desire to be.

Our imagination is powerful! If we would learn to use it for good instead of allowing garbage to consume it, we all would be better off and a lot happier. Imagination is a part of our minds. Our mind is where creation begins. In order to fulfill something great in our lives, we must first be able to visualize it! Imagination is necessary if you are to walk by faith, for it is the ability to form a mental image of something that is not perceived through the five senses. The greatest aspect of manifesting our desires is to act like the thing that we are imagining is real and already made manifest.

Our problem is that we imagine how bad a situation is or could be and/or what we don't have and this kind of active imagination is creating unwanted circumstances and situations. When we hold a thought or imagine something long enough, we will produce the harvest of that which we are focused on. So make every imagined thought count! Every great idea and/or invention started with a thought in someone's imagination! So start imagining!

MOOD CHANGER

"Finally, brethren, whatsoever things are true, whatsoever things are honest, whatsoever things are just, whatsoever things are pure, whatsoever things are lovely, whatsoever things are of good report; if there be any virtue, and if there be any praise, think on these things." –Philippians 4:8

Its been scientifically proven that people have the power to change the world around them simply with the use of their thoughts, words and emotions. One very popular experiment done that proves this theory was performed by Dr. Masaru Emoto whereby he found by placing varying words (of both positive and negative energies) on jars of water (i.e. you make me sick, thank you) and freezing it, the container with the positive words formed a beautiful crystal, whereas the container with the negative words formed a very distorted looking crystal. So what does this say about us and the words we speak daily to each other, or those who are in our lives?

What affects are we having on each other and ourselves, considering that the human body is made up of 60% water? Something to think about!

We must begin to speak positive words, find ways to keep our thoughts in a positive state. If you are having trouble in this area, just put on some uplifting music, for this has also been shown to change our frequency so that we are attracting only those things we desire into our lives. This is why affirmations are so powerful! By stating positive words over your life repetitiously, your mind will begin to ultimately believe it and that which we believe...we will become! Bottom line...change your mood...change your reality!

HOW TO MEDITATE

"This book of the law shall not depart out of thy mouth; but thou shalt meditate therein day and night, that thou mayest observe to do according to all that is written therein: for then thou shalt make thy way prosperous, and then thou shalt have good success." –Joshua 1:8

Meditation is key to hearing from God and receiving instructions as to how to go about accomplishing goals, visions and dreams. Many of us get caught up in the day-to-day stresses of life never finding time to relax. This is what satan wants. The more busy you become, the less time with God you will have. The less time with God you have, the more unlikely it is that you will accomplish your goals, or maybe you will but you will never have peace or be in position to enjoy the fruit of your labor.

Our culture and society teaches us that the harder you work the better off you'll be. This is the furthest thing from the truth according to Psalm 127:2 "It is useless for you to work so hard from early morning to late at night, anxiously working for food to eat; for God gives rest to His loved ones." We must learn how to hear God's instructions for our lives in order to live happy, purpose filled lives! Many of us are working jobs we despise, creating frustration, stress, bitterness and resentment, all the fruit of the adversary. This negativity breeds more circumstances and situations in our lives that create more stress and frustrations...its a vicious cycle. So find what you love and DO IT!

In order to find what you love, meditate! Ask God what He would have you to do. Our purpose is always tied up into our passion. So what are you passionate about? You may be asking...so how do I find what I'm passionate about? Your passion is something you are willing to do without being paid to do it! It will be something that motivates you to wake up everyday. If you are still unsure, meditate, get some alone time with God and ask Him. He will lead and guide you.

Make sure to stay clear of ungodly meditation (i.e. yoga) I was surprised to find that so many believers practice this demonic ritual. Yoga taps into the demonic realm and other Hindu gods. As believers we are to refrain from meditating on anything that takes us away from God according to Exodus 20:3 "you shall have no other gods before me." God makes it clear that we are to meditate on His Word. With so many vices in the world fighting for our attention we must discipline ourselves to come away from that which is not beneficial and focus our attention and energy on things that will be an asset to our lives instead of a liability.

BENEFITS OF MEDITATION

Stress reduction
Enhance concentration levels
Brings happiness
Retards the aging process
Peace
Allows for greater understanding
Yields self control

So remember Philippians 4:8 "Finally, brethren, whatsoever things are true, whatsoever things are honest, whatsoever things are just, whatsoever things are pure, whatsoever things are lovely, whatsoever things are of good report; if there be any virtue, and if there be any praise, think on these things." Or you can say meditate on these things. This scripture is a great place to start if you are unsure as to where to direct your thoughts. Keep in mind that meditating is creating so make your meditation time count!

DECREES & DECLARATIONS

"Thou shalt also decree a thing, and it shall be established unto thee: and the light shall shine upon thy ways."
—Job 22:28

Our words have POWER! But what good is it if we don't know how to use them? "Words with no direction, is like shooting and arrow with no target" –Lucindy Lumu. We must teach ourselves how to speak with intention. Our words shape our reality. How is this so? When God created us in His image, with that came dominion. Dominion is "authority". So the reason we are able to decree a thing and it be established unto us, is because of the "authority" that has been given to us by God. So we must now understand what a decree is. A decree is an *official order* issued by a legal authority. There is the word "authority" again. God is really trying to get us to realize how powerful we really are. So when we put it all together, we understand that we have legal authority under God to give official orders!

Decrees are like affirmations except with Power! Affirmations are not bad, but if you really want to see change happen on your behalf, learn how to decree a thing over your life. This kind of authority and power cannot be given by man or taken away by man. It is a God given authority! God has put us in positions of power as His children, its part of our inheritance.

The beauty is we can exercise it whenever the enemy is coming against us in our families, on our jobs, in our minds and/or in our society. Our authority is not limited to people, culture, society or people holding worldly positions of authority. I understand that judges, police officers, lawyers and /or presidents of the U.S can be intimidating; they were trained to make us feel that way. What I am trying to get you to realize is, we also, are in positions of authority and our positions are more powerful simply because our position was not man given. God is all powerful and the only one we should fear, Matthew 10:28

states, "and fear not them which kill the body, but are not able to kill the soul: but rather fear Him which is able to destroy both soul and body in hell." We were created to be MORE than conquerors! When you are being falsely accused, attacked unjustly...decree that NO WEAPON FORMED AGAINST YOU SHALL PROSPER! –Isaiah 54:17.

Now that we understand what a decree is, what is a declaration? A declaration is closer to an affirmation. In that its like an announcement or a statement. We can declare who we are in Christ. For example: I AM THE RIGHTEOUSNESS OF GOD. I AM HEALED. These are declarations. By using the words DECREE AND DECLARE IN FRONT OF OUR statements and orders, we summons the power of God! Change your language and begin to incorporate these 2 powerful, life changing words into your prayer time and I guarantee you'll see the hand of God!

SOWING AND REAPING

"Give, and it shall be given unto you; good measure, pressed down, and shaken together, and running over, shall men give into your bosom...." –Luke 6:38

A farmer knows that if he wants to produce a harvest of apples, he must sow apple seeds. Many of you are reading this in hopes of learning how to manifest abundance in your life. My response to you would be just like the farmer, you must sow that which you desire in order to reap the harvest. So if its money you need, sow money. There are so many ways you can sow money. Church is not the only place you can sow financial seeds. You can sow in your favorite charity, you can bless a family in need, you can sow into someone else's vision or dream. There are many ways guys to give, so there is no excuse. How can you expect money if you don't sow/give money? Does a farmer anticipate a harvest if there is no seed in the ground?

This law of sowing and reaping is a universal law and will work no matter who applies it. Just like the law of gravity...gravity doesn't care who you are, its going to work regardless. We can also apply the law of sowing and reaping with love, if you desire for people to respond to you in love, try being loving. Give love away and love will come back to you. Same goes for hate, sow seeds of hate, hate will find its way into your life. Be mindful of the seeds you are sowing.

I know we've been trained to be selfish and to think in a selfish way. Most of us think if we give something like money, away, we won't get it back, or we won't have enough. With God it's the total opposite! The MORE you give, the MORE you receive according to Malachi 3:10 "Bring the whole tithe into the storehouse, that there may be food in my house. Test me in this, says the Lord almighty, and see if I will not throw open the floodgates of heaven and pour out so much blessing that there will not be room enough to store it." By the way, this is the only area of our lives that God tells us to TEST Him in. Just sayin, funny how the one area we want to be stingy over, is the very area God instructs us to test Him in.

We don't trust God in this area of our lives because we lack faith and we've been programmed under a poverty way of thinking. If you have trouble giving and are stingy, selfish, and always thinking in terms of NOT enough...you have a poverty mentality and you are in need of some reprogramming! This kind of stinkin thinkin is hindering the blessings from flowing into your life.

Sowing/giving requires training, you have to train yourself to be a giver and I'm not talking about a giver of things you care nothing about. True giving comes from sacrifice. Once you've trained yourself to be a sacrificial giver, it will become second nature to you. Luke 12:34 states: "For where your treasure is, their will your heart be also." Keep in mind we attract what we feel. If you feel broke, you will attract lack. If you feel abundance, you will attract wealth. Keep your focus away from that which you don't want and turn your attention to that which you do want. So sow/give freely and I guarantee, you will reap freely and abundantly!

BELIEVE

"If you believe, you will receive whatever you ask for in prayer."
Matthew 21:22

You must understand that you control what comes and goes in your life. God can only bless you according to your level of faith as we read over in Matthew 9:29 "...according to your faith let it be done unto you." Faith and belief are trust issues. If you find that you lack faith or the ability to believe God's Word, you will find that you have trust issues with God. Some clergy and psychologist have mentioned that this can stem from trust issues with our biological fathers, thus not being able to trust God.

As a person who didn't have the best relationship with my father, I totally saw the negative effects being played out in my work relationships, personal relationships and ultimately in my relationship with God. I realized later in life that I don't have to allow that to affect me. I can choose to shift my entire paradigm.

The way I broke away from that negativity and mindset was turning my life over to God. As I drew closer to God, He began to reveal himself to me. He became my father, friend and confidant. Whenever I was in need, He met those needs. The more I embraced Him, the more I felt His presence in my life, thus, the more I believed.

He took care of me when I had no one. He provided for me, loved me, and protected me. After all He's done for me...I just sit back and reflect on His goodness towards me and it's easy for me to believe. He hasn't failed me yet!

Another way that has helped with my unbelief is His Word. Romans 10:17 "So then faith cometh by hearing, and hearing by the Word of God." In order for our conscious and subconscious mind to be renewed and reprogrammed with the things we want to see made manifest in our lives, we must hear and speak those things repeatedly. Scientists have proven that the more you hear something and speak something repetitiously, the more you begin to believe it! Again, just pointing out why it's important to guard your thoughts and words. Thoughts create. Beliefs are thoughts. What you think about or what you believe about...YOU CREATE!

CONFLICT

"My brethren, count it all joy when ye fall into divers
temptations; knowing this, that the trying of your faith worketh
patience. But let patience have her perfect work, that ye may be
perfect and entire, wanting nothing."
James 1:2-4

Part of getting through conflict successfully and

what I mean by successfully is without bitterness,

resentment hatred and hopelessness; we must understand

that we have a heavenly Father that will fight our battles for

us. There is really no need to get worked up over something

that is not our battle. Our job is to stay positive while God

works on our behalf. Its not always easy, but if we train our

thoughts where to go and keep our words few, we'll see the

hand of God show up on our behalf more often.

Understand that conflict is necessary in order to

build our character. Godly character is what allows us to

handle the blessings of God. Have you ever seen what

happens to people with bad character who come from

poverty and they are given an overwhelming amount of money at one time? It destroys them! They're selfish, stingy and rude! So before God brings His children into "His" blessings He must first test our character in order to prove that we're capable of handling all He has in store for us. I'm a firm believer in turning my conflict into currency by allowing God to use me while I'm going through difficult times.

This could be done in so many ways, for example, being a listening ear, offering words of encouragement or just being that support system for others during your difficult time. You may be asking how does this translate into currency? Remember Giving is receiving. The law of sowing and reaping reminds us that if we give we receive a harvest multiplied over. When our giving is done sacrificially its more beneficial. Most of us want to do the opposite during our difficult time. But I urge you to look for people to bless. As you're busy being a blessing to someone else, God is busy using people to be a blessing to you. Sowing and reaping...IT NEVER FAILS!

DIRECTION

"Trust in the Lord with all thine heart; and lean not unto thine own understanding. In all thy ways acknowledge Him and He shall direct thy paths." –Proverbs 3:5-6

Direction is key to getting where you want to be in life. Unfortunately, most of have no idea what direction to take. This is why relationship with God is most important. As stated in the above scripture, God will direct our paths, if we trust in Him. He is always waiting for our command according to Isaiah 45:11. Our heavenly Father delights in blessing His children. He has even equipped us with our own personal assistants. These assistants are called angels. He commands them to guard us in all our ways according to Psalm 91:11. Which is why we should never feel alone. Angels are just one way God speaks to us.

Another way is through our instincts or intuition. How we feel about something is usually a great indicator as to which direction we should take. Bad feelings usually mean, do not proceed, whereas, good feelings typically mean proceed.

You may ask, what if I have mixed feelings? Great question! This means to proceed with caution. God is always exposing us to signs that will indicate if we are going in the right direction. Signs are all around us. This is why we must be in tuned in with the Holy Spirit in order to see and hear what God is saying. Our intuition is God speaking through us. Signs and clues is God speaking around us.

When in doubt, ask. Get some alone time with God and seek His face for answers. I've always received clarity after sitting in the presence of God. Sometimes the clarity could come in the form of a direct answer, prophetic word, song and/or an inspired idea. It's important to act on the inspired ideas, because from it yields your blessing. Every inspired idea I've acted upon yielded increase. I had to train myself to act on the inspired ideas instead of blowing them off, which is what a lot of us tend to do. Doing this prevents blessings from entering into your life. We must fellowship with God, listen and act in order to receive.

CREATING WITH GOD

"I tell you the truth, anyone who believes in me will do the same works I have done, and even greater works, because I am going to be with the Father. You can ask for anything in my name, and I will do it, so that the Son can bring Glory to the Father." –John 14:12-13

Jesus is our representative. God made it clear that no one can come to Him accept through His son according to John 14:6. If we are going to create, we must be connected to a power source. As believers, our power source is Christ. This is why we end our prayers or petitions with, "in Jesus name." The Son of God is always seeking ways to bring glory to the Father and His method is through us. God cannot fulfill His plans in the earth without a willing vessel. We should be ready and willing to be used by God. By living out the Word of God, we allow God to use us and bless us. Our faith is our currency that allows us to create the extraordinary lives we dream of.

STAYING MOTIVATED & REPROGRAMMING THE SUBCONSCIOUS MIND

"And be not conformed to this world: but be ye transformed by the renewing of your mind, that ye may prove what is that good, and acceptable and perfect will of God."
Romans 12:2

Our minds are the central station from which all things are birthed which is why we are instructed to renew the mind. Ways we can renew our mind is through what we see, hear, speak and read *continuously*. After learning how powerful our minds really are, I became very sensitive as to what I digested audibly and visually. Because our subconscious mind is where our habits form and where we carry out our beliefs and behaviors, I begin to saturate my subconscious mind with subliminal declarations and scriptures surrounding wealth, love and peace. These were the areas of my life that needed reprogramming. I chose subliminal declarations and scriptures because scientists have proven that the subconscious mind receives information that the conscious mind cannot perceive and then stores it. If the information being received is repeated enough, the subconscious mind will begin to believe it and thoughts, feelings and behaviors will become a part of who we are. The subconscious mind cannot tell the difference between what is reality and what is not! Which is why we must be careful what we program it to believe! Whatever you place in your subconscious mind, it has no choice but to manifest!

So for example: if you have a problem with health, listen to subliminal scriptures on healing while you are sleeping every night for at least 21 days. Subliminals bypass our conscious mind and reprogram our subconscious mind. Experts say it takes 21-30 days to break a habit or to create a new belief. So why not take 30 days to shift your paradigm and create a new and intentional belief system? Its in our best interest to impress upon our subconscious mind with messages we want to see made manifest in our lives, such as wealth, good health, love and more. Remember, what we sow audibly, visually or with our words we will reap a harvest.

I love doing my chores while listening to lectures or positive declarations on success, wealth and happiness. This is where my motivation comes from. I have a playlist of lectures, books and/or affirmations that I allow to play throughout my day to keep me reminded of who I am and how powerful my mind and words are. This is an excellent way to stay focused and positive. These practices are a part of my daily routine.

GREED & PRIDE

"What good is for someone to gain the whole world, yet forfeit their soul?" –Mark 8:36

It has been said that we can't out give God. More surprisingly, in the Word of God, the only scripture where God instructs us to test Him is in the area of our money. If we look at Malachi 3:10 it states, "Bring all the tithes into the storehouse so there will be enough food in my Temple. If you do, says the Lord of Heaven's Armies, I will open the windows of heaven for you. I will pour out a blessing so great you won't have enough room to take it in! Try it! Put me to the test!" If we believe God, why do we have such a hard time letting go of our money? Why do we fear losing something that God instructs us to give away?

I personally believe that people have a wrong perception of giving. People's perception of money is tied to the state of their hearts.

When our hearts are turned towards God we walk by faith
and are generous as our heavenly Father is generous,
however, when our hearts are turned away from God we
walk in fear and selfishness. When we give, we activate the
law of sowing and reaping that yields abundance, the caveat
is also true, when we decide to walk in selfishness, we reap
lack and poverty.

Greed has never been proven to make anyone
happy. Greed has ruined people, families and businesses.
According to Proverbs 15:27 "the greedy brings ruin to
their households, but those who hate bribes will live."
Because we are human our flesh is always at war with God.
The flesh is never satisfied according to Proverbs 27:20.
Knowing this, we as believers should always work to
crucify our flesh with prayer AND fasting in order to keep
our motives and hearts pure towards God. In doing this, we
can assure our desires are in line with our creator!

Living in a culture that is constantly comparing everyone against the next one, I understand that it is hard not to fall victim to wanting to keep up, but be very careful that you don't become ensnared by envy and pride! For pride comes before the fall according to Proverbs 16:18 and

a heart at peace gives life to the body, but envy rots the bones according to Proverbs 14:30.

LIFE MORE ABUNDANTLY

"The thief does not come except to steal, and to kill, and to destroy. I have come that they may have life, and that they may have it more abundantly." -John 10:10

It is imperative that we understand God's purpose behind abundance. Abundance simply means a very large quantity of something. So in knowing this, we can now restate John 10:10 to read: The thief does not come except to steal, and to kill, and to destroy. I have come that they may have life, and that they may have it in *large quantities*! God never advocates for lack or poverty! So many people in the religious communities have been brainwashed into thinking that lack and poverty makes one more holy or righteous, when it's actually the opposite. Let's just take a look at the Word of God and what it says about prosperity:

Deuteronomy 8:18 "But thou shalt remember the Lord thy God: for it is He that giveth thee power to create wealth, that

He may establish His covenant which He sware unto thy fathers, as it is this day".

3 John 1:2 "Beloved, I wish above all things that thou mayest prosper and be in health, even as thy soul prospereth".

2 Corinthians 8:9 "For ye know the grace of our Lord Jesus Christ, that, though He was rich, yet for your sakes He became poor, that ye through His poverty might be rich".

So we can conclude from the scriptures that God wants us to live a prosperous life both in health and in wealth. There is no need to walk in poverty when Jesus already carried that out for us on the cross so that we don't have to! There's no need to walk in sickness and disease when Jesus already bore our infirmities on the cross. Its like God is instructing us to live an abundant life through Him!

Why then, do so many of us walk in lack? Whether its in our finances, health or relationships. I strongly feel this deprived mindset comes from an auto-generated mindset that has been programmed to carry out thoughts and actions that are void of abundance. We must realize that in order to believe in the abundance that God speaks of in His Word, we must first believe. In order to believe we must reprogram our minds daily or as the Word of God states, we must renew our minds daily. And the way we renew our minds daily is through daily meditations for our conscious minds and nightly meditations for our subconscious mind, which we will look more into in a later chapter. Both meditation processes are necessary in order to believe and attract wealth into our life. Joshua 1:8 prove this by instructing us to meditate on God's Word both day and night.

CREATING CHILD LIKE FAITH

"Children are like wet cement whatever falls on them makes an impression" –Haim Ginott

Ever notice you never have to tell a small child to believe? When we as parents tell our children that we are going to do something for them or give them something, it's amazing how they naturally believe. There's no question, no doubt...just belief.

Take note to how the child responds. They respond with such excitement and enthusiasm. You never see small children worrying about if we as parents will keep our word and fulfill the desired thing or action. They carryon as if it's already done! And so shall we be in our faith as adults. We should receive whatever God has promised us or whatever we are desiring to attract into our lives with enthusiasm and excitement, carryon as if it already happened and not worry ourselves with whether or not its going to happen.

HOW TO CREATE AND
MAINTAIN HAPPINESS

"For every minute you are angry you lose sixty seconds of
happiness" –Ralph Waldo Emerson

Happiness is what we all long for. Happiness is
something that we all strive to attain, but why then, is being
happy so difficult for so many of us? It is my belief that the
state of being happy can only come from our Creator. I say
this because it's our Creator, that not only created you and
I, but Created this emotion that we call happiness. Let's
prove it! We are all human beings. I think we can all agree
to that...if not, then this book is not for you...lol! According
to Acts 17:28 "For in Him we live, and move and have our
being...". So if our being is in Him, then we can conclude
that it is in Him our happiness resides. Romans 15:13 states
"Now the God of hope fill you with all joy and peace in
believing, that ye may abound in hope, through the power
of the Holy Ghost". This scripture gives us all we need in
order to manifest any desire into our life. It tells us who's

the source of our happiness which is the emotion needed in creating our desires and it also confirms that God, who is our source, will give us the ability to believe which is also vital in attracting those things that be not...into our lives.

Now in order to tap into the joy of the Lord and live out true happiness, you must be found in Him. In order to connect to the God source you must commit your life to Him and invite Him in as your personal Lord and Savior. As believers, we call this process "salvation". Just by reading the following prayer you will be saved!

Heavenly Father,

I come to you in prayer asking for the forgiveness of my sins. I confess with my mouth and believe with my heart that Jesus is your Son, and that He died on the cross at calvary that I might be forgiven and have eternal life in the Kingdom of Heaven. Father, I believe that Jesus rose from the dead and I ask your right now to come into my life right now and be my personal Lord and Savior. I repent of my sins and

will worship you all the days of my life! Because

your Word is truth, I confess with my mouth that I am born again

and cleansed by the blood of Jesus! In Jesus name amen.

Praise God! Now that you are saved, the real fun begins! First thing to remember: you are NOT alone! When test and trials come to get you down, turn inwards and pray that the Holy Spirit give you peace and joy in your current situation. You must then take action to maintain it.

WAYS TO MAINTAIN HAPPINESS:

1. **MUSIC:** I enjoy listening to positive and uplifting music. Music that is inspiring always puts me in a good mood and shifts my focus from the negative things that are trying to take my joy and puts it back on Jesus and the positive things that I am looking forward to.

2. **Fellowship:** Fellowship with friends is a great way to maintain happiness. Our friends can help get our minds off of the negative things that may be going on in our lives. They also can serve as a great source of encouragement! This is a good source only if your friends are not negative, then it will defeat the purpose! Also fellowshipping with your church is also a way to stay plugged in to God and draw strength and happiness from the saints of God.

3. **Staying Active:** By staying active in your daily activities (i.e. sports, exercising, work, hobbies) we keep our minds active on the positive things that we are occupied with. Staying active forces us to focus on our goals and helps us to remember that there is more to life than focusing on negative things. Being occupied is an excellent way to maintain happiness.

4. **Prayer:** Prayer is always a sure way to maintain happiness! Just by communicating what's on your heart and mind to your Creator will shift your spirit (energy) to a much more happier place. You will get a sense of relief and peace immediately. I find when I vent to God I notice a calming presence that envelopes me, and miraculously the issue that seemed so bad, now don't seem so bad. Isaiah 26:3 explains this phenomenon by promising us that "You will keep in perfect peace all who trust in you, all whose thoughts are fixed on you"

5. **Meditation:** Biblical meditation is very powerful and relaxing. By getting alone and quiet and setting your mind on God's promises, and visualizing your desires, you will find yourself full of peace and happiness. This is a sure way to draw those things you desire into your life as well!

Joshua 1:8 confirm this by stating, "Study this book of instruction continually. Meditate on it day and night so you will be sure to obey everything written in it. Only then will you prosper and succeed in all you do".

YOUR PASSION IS YOUR PURPOSE

"A man's gift maketh room for him, and bringeth him before great men"
-Proverbs 18:16

My Pastor once explained that your passion is anything you enjoy doing that nobody has to pay you for! I find this to be one of the best explanations to the age-old question, how do I find my passion?

So many of us tend to confuse making a lot of money with purpose. There are so many people working financially fulfilling careers who are unhappy. The key words here are "financially fulfilling". Financial abundance has nothing to do with "self" fulfillment or happiness. One may argue that they are happy because of their wealth, which I have yet to meet someone with that declaration. Keep in mind that things such as wealth and material possessions only bring temporary fulfillment and satisfaction. So loving money and material possessions only last but a moment, because possessions and money cannot reciprocate love nor can they fill the void of the purpose you were created on this earth to fulfill.

Your gift will make room for you as stated in Proverbs. It is important that you find out what you are gifted at and pursue it! As my pastor use to say, "if you chase your passion, money will begin to chase you." It is in your gift that you will find your purpose! Your passion is tied to your gift! What excites you? What brings you joy more than anything? What are you most comfortable at doing? If you can answer these questions, then you can honestly say you have found your purpose my dear friend.

Congratulations!

THERE ARE NO COINCIDENSES

"And we know that all things work together for good to them
that love God, to them who are the called according to His
purpose"
-Romans 8:28

We are all connected! Spiritually speaking, we are all created in the image of God our creator according to Genesis 1:27. Physicists have confirmed this molecular connection and refer to it as Quantum Entanglement, which by definition states this very truth. This is why we must be mindful how we treat one another, because what we do to others we ultimately do to ourselves!

All things happen for a reason. Our thoughts, emotions and words are the reasons things happen. God has already given us an expected end according to Jeremiah 29:11 that tell us "For I know the thoughts that I think towards you, saith the Lord, thoughts of peace and not of evil, to give you an expected end". If God already has our expected end in place, we must align ourselves with His purpose for our lives in order to receive it. We do this by feeling, thinking, speaking and acting like our Creator. We start by feeling and embracing His love. Next we think on whatsoever things are true, honest, just, pure, lovely and are of good report. Third we are to speak those things that be not as though they are and last we are called to walk as Christ walked according to 1 John 2:6. This is the moment where you will begin to realize that coincidence is no longer coincidence but rather expectation! In following through with these steps we can be reassured that we are divinely aligned with our Creator and can expect that which He desires for us, to be made manifest in our lives!

THOUGH IT TARRIES

"For the vision is yet for an appointed time, but at the end it shall
speak, and not lie: though it tarry, wait for it; because it will
surely come, it will not tarry"
-Habakkuk 2:3

I come across so many people who give up before they've had the chance to experience the blessing. Our American culture has done a great job imprinting on the minds of its inhabitants that things in life are suppose to happen quickly. Let's look at our food; we want fast food. When we're at home, we microwave our food. We gotta have the fastest wi-fi connection and the list goes on. Our culture today is obsessed over having things quickly and without waiting. We have been trained to be impatient! So it's no wonder why so many people don't have faith. Faith requires patience. You must be willing to wait for the vision to come to pass. Whenever patience is omitted from faith, vision is omitted from life. There is a saying that says, good things come to those who wait. I feel this statement compliments Habakkuk 2:3 very well.

I understand the anxiety that can come into play as we wait for our visions to be made manifest, but you must trust God who promises that it will surely come. Therefore, do not give place to anxiousness. According to Philipians 4:6-7 God instructs us to "be anxious for nothing..." I like to think of the waiting process like ordering fast food. When we are ordering, sometimes we get in ridiculous long lines without complaining and we WAIT. We wait to pull up to the ordering speaker. We wait to pull up to the first window to pay for our order and then we wait to receive our food. Never once do we get anxious over the possibility of not receiving our food. We sit there AS IF we already have it! And this my friends, is the mindset and attitude we must operate in, in order to manifest our visions. Its really that simple. So, relax and know that it is on the way!

VISION

"Where there is no vision, the people perish..."
Proverbs 29:18

We live in a world where a small percent of people are actually living out there dreams for their lives. Most people fall into careers for money, convenience or because someone else told them what to do. It is rare that you will find those in the workforce or in careers because of passion or because it was their vision. As a result, these people, studies have shown are more prone to stress, sickness, anger, frustration and depression. We were never designed to pursue money, convenience or someone else's vision for our lives. We were, however, designed to fulfill God's purpose for our unique lives! God has put His purpose in each and every one of us. This is why success apart from God leaves us unfulfilled. There is still a void, feelings of non- accomplishment and a feeling of emptiness. This is because success without God is meaningless! The Word of God tells us that "your gifts will make room for you..." according to Proverbs 18:16. Find out what your gifts are and chase them and I promise everything of monetary value will chase you as a result.

Vision and purpose go hand in hand. Once these two are realized then you have successfully found the meaning to your life. It is through vision and purpose we have hope. Which is why without them people perish because if purpose is unrealized and vision is unfulfilled, then hope is non-existent and once hope is non-existant then life perishes. So pray and ask God to reveal to you your purpose. Visualize it daily, set goals to accomplish it, act on it and fulfill your destiny!

INSPIRED ACTION

"Even so faith, if it hath not works, is dead, being alone"
-James 2:17

It would be nice if all we had to do were speak, think and feel things into our lives; however, this is not always the case. In most cases and I say most cases because there are things that we can attract into our lives without effort. For example, have you ever thought about someone and wondered how they were doing and then all of a sudden they call you, well this is an example of the power of thought, emotion and visualization. However, inspired action requires more effort on our end. Inspired action is an action that comes to us through our intuition, impulse or other means. Its your ah-ha moment, that moment that just feels right and so you go for it! An inspired action doesn't feel burdensome or daunting! It actually feels...inspiring!

For example, you may want more income, however, you

don't want a 9-5 job. You may get an inspired idea to start your own business. All of sudden details of how to start the business start being downloaded into your memory. Now you are inspired and excited to start this new business venture. Another example would be that you need more income and you hear an inner voice tell you to apply at a particular place. So as a result of you listening to this inner voice, you go to that particular place, apply for the job and you get hired. These are examples of inspired action. These can also be summed up as works! So as stated in the scripture, faith without works is dead.

We must take inspired action if we want to manifest the desires of our hearts. Our dreams, visions and desires will not just drop into our laps. So learn how to pay attention to your intuition. Listen to the voice of God and step out on faith!

NOT GOOD ENOUGH

"Not of works, lest any man should boast"
-Ephesians 2:9

We must constantly remind ourselves to stay away from stinkin thinkin. Having thoughts of self-defeat, not being good enough, not measuring up or even staying in a mindset of constantly comparing ourselves to others only breeds discontentment and defeat. This energy or spirit will continue in your life unless you change it. Your attitude towards yourself is key to manifesting your desires or fears. Keep in mind, we attract what we feel, think and speak, be it positive or negative.

There is not one man greater than the other. Our greatness comes from our Creator and it is in Christ who we have our existence. This is why no man should boast! If you are going to boast, boast on the Creator of all living things, the God who created the universe, the heavens and the earth and not on those who have no heaven or hell to put you in! So stop with the comparisons! God created you fearfully and wonderfully according to Psalm 139:14 and there is nothing you can't accomplish once you put your mind to it.

If God put in you a vision and a dream then that means you are good enough and qualified to make it manifest in your life but you must believe you can achieve it. Listening to positive meditations while sleeping at night as well as meditating on the Word of God while awake helps renew your thinking by replacing negative thoughts with positive ones. By changing your thoughts, you'll change your outcomes.

REPROGRAMMING THE SUBCONSCIENCE MIND

"In a dream, in a vision of the night, when deep sleep falleth upon men, in slumberings upon the bed; then he openth the ears of men, and sealeth their instructions "
-Job 33:15-16

Our subconscious mind is where it all goes down. Our behaviors, mindsets, patterns and automatic responses come from our subconscious mind. For example, we do not have to tell our heart to beat or our eyes to blink when needed, these actions are on autopilot by way of our subconscious mind. Our learned behaviors come from our subconscious mind.

Our subconscious mind cannot tell the difference between what is real and what is not. This is why when we have a dream that seem real and we wake up in a cold sweat and are experiencing rapid breathing as if we were literally experiencing that dream, this is due to our subconscious mind. This is how powerful the subconscious mind is.

Every word, idea or attitude that was done repetitiously in our lives since childhood has left an imprint on our subconscious mind and has become a part of who we are. The subconscious mind is a collection of commands and repetitions that got programmed over time. So if you are struggling with poverty and living paycheck to paycheck, this is a learned behavior and belief. As children, we hear our parents say, we're on a budget, we don't have enough, we're broke or we can't afford this or that, these repeated declarations became embedded into your subconscious mind shaping who you are as a person and your attitude towards money and wealth or the lack thereof. This is why lack is an automatic behavior and mindset in your life.

Nobody have to teach you how to be broke. The opposite is true, however, for those that are wealthy and live an abundant life. Wealth is their mindset because they were either trained growing up that they had more than enough and that they are wealthy or if they didn't grow up with this mindset, they reprogrammed their subconscious mind in order to believe this way. These kinds of positive affirmations being declared for years in the life of a child will create a healthy mindset towards wealth and money. Therefore, money will flow to them easily and effortlessly as adults. So the great news is that our subconscious mind can be reprogrammed so that we are able to have the right attitudes and mindsets towards money, people and life in general.

According to Romans 12:2 "And be not conformed to this world: but be ye transformed by the renewing of your mind..."in order to become the person you desire, the person you envision, you must renew your mind. Your thoughts transform you into whatever it is you're focusing on. That's how powerful your thoughts are. So if you have old thoughts of I can't and I'll never then you won't and you never will. In the words of Henry Ford, "If you think you can, you're right, if you think you can't, you're right.

The choice is yours. God instructs us where to keep our thoughts over in Philipians 4:8. So if we are not keeping our thoughts on things that are lovely, honest, noble and of good report then we are more than likely focusing and entertaining negative thoughts, thus creating and attracting negative situations and circumstances.

Joshua 1:8 also instructs us to meditate both day and night on the Word of God. Because whatever we listen to before we fall into deep sleep gets sealed as stated in Job 33:16, its best to be sure the right instructions are being sealed or locked in just before bed. What I do is I listen to my playlist of meditations at night while I'm sleeping. I have a guided meditation that plays a combination of positive affirmations and scriptures. I do this every night. This constant repetition is reprogramming my subconscious mind, therefor, new ways of thinking, new attitudes and behaviors are being developed and sealed in.

So if you find that you have a wrong attitude towards money or health, I suggest listening to meditations at night that consist of scriptures on healing or finances along with positive affirmations on healing and money. I find this to be the fastest way to reprogram the subconscious mind. Let the meditations play while you are sleeping for 21-30 days. Scientists have stated that it takes at a minimum, 21 days to break a habit or create a new belief. The subconscious mind is reprogrammed through repetition! So it's strongly advised that you put in the work on your subconscious mind if you want to achieve positive results.

HOW TO INCREASE YOUR FAITH

"If ye have faith as a grain of mustard seed, ye shall say unto this
mountain, remove hence to yonder place; and it shall remove;
and nothing shall be impossible unto you"
-Matthew 17:20

If you struggle in having faith and manifesting

things in your life, it's good to start with believing for

something small. They way you will go about this is by first

recognizing that we attract things to ourselves according to

our beliefs, that's what faith is. Our beliefs remember are

our thoughts. So focus your attention on something that you

want that is easy for you to believe. This can be as small as

a cup of coffee. You will start by telling yourself it would

be nice to have a cup of coffee. Then visualize yourself

with that cup of coffee. Make your visualizations as vivid

as possible by including your 5 senses: smell, touch, taste,

hear and sight. Once you visualize yourself already having

this cup of coffee, tell God thank you for blessing you with such an awesome cup of coffee, then forget about it. Once you manifest the coffee in your life, write it down and keep a journal. Congratulations, you just activated your faith! By journaling and keeping track of your manifestations, you see the power of God working through you and this gives you the confidence you need to believe for something greater.

MY LOA SUCCESS STORY

"Now faith is the substance of things hoped for, the evidence of
things not seen"
Hebrews 11:1

I can recall the time when I first learned about the
law of attraction and thinking to myself, this ain't nothing
but implementing faith, it can't be that easy. And so began
my discovery of how easy or not easy this thing called law
of attraction really is.

So as a stay at home mom, I really didn't desire
anything serious, but I had some things in mind that I
wouldn't mind having. So I created a vision board on my
laptop in September of 2015. My husband new nothing
about what I had been researching let alone this virtual
vision board that I created. So keep that in mind. I wanted
to first make sure that it worked and that I knew what I was
doing. So I placed on my vision board a picture of a new
office to do all my makeup and hair tutorials, a canon t5i
camera, a rose gold iphone, and a new wardrobe. I figured

what do I have to lose, why not put everything on there that I felt I wanted at the time. After constructing this vision board, every day I would go down stairs in our basement and began declaring these things into my life. After I would declare them in my life, every day after that was spent thanking God for bringing them into my life. I would also go to bed every night with headphones on listening to meditation affirmations on wealth over the course of 3 months. I found after about 3 months, I just let it go. I didn't give up in frustration; I just let it go and said if it happens it happens. This attitude is key! I didn't worry about the how. I was content if it happened or if it didn't. It was 3 months later in March, so a total of 6 months from the time I started this process, that my husband came to me and said God told him to invest in my work! He then went on to tell me that he was going to purchase me a new office and purchase the camera I had been hoping for. As if it couldn't get any better, he took me to get the rose gold phone I wanted that was on my vision board and to top it all off, he blessed me with a new wardrobe as well! All this manifested within 6 months. I was floored. I eventually revealed to my husband my vision board and what I had learned about manifesting and law of attraction and he was just as shocked as I was. He asked me to show him how and so began his journey to walk by faith *"on purpose"* and dominion!

ATTITUDE OF GRATITUDE

"And whatsoever ye do in word or deed, do all in the name of the
Lord Jesus, giving thanks to God and the Father by him"
-Colossians 3:17

Our attitudes can either work for us or against us.
Most times it is our attitudes that are responsible for the
unwanted things and/or people in our lives. We must
remember that attitudes are energy. Our emotions and how
we feel towards things, situations and people is the fuel that
attracts these things to us. Emotions are our energy in
motion. By having an attitude of gratitude we are already
setting in motion to attract blessing to us. Gratitude
communicates to God that we already have it. If you recall,
God instructs us in the scriptures that we are to speak those
things that be not as though they are according to Romans
4:17. This is done by having an attitude of gratitude and
being thankful for already having those things in our lives.
We should live our lives in this mindset daily.

Everyday we should be thankful for not only the things that are presently in our lives but for the things we cannot see. In doing so, we train our spirit man to walk by faith and not by sight. The more we operate in the attitude of gratitude, the faster things will be made manifest in our lives. Gratitude comes from love and love is the highest frequency according to scientist that we are able to attract good things unto ourselves. This doesn't surprise me because God is love! According to James 1:17 "every good and perfect gift comes from above, and cometh down from the Father..."

After prayer, I enjoy listening to gratitude meditations in the morning upon waking up because it sets the course of my day and put my spirit in position to receive.

LAW OF DETACHMENT

"When I stop struggling, I float"
-Unknown

The law of detachment says that in order to successfully attract something, you must be detached to the outcome. Letting go of our expectations, I believe, is by far one of the hardest aspects of faith. People are constantly asking the question, how do I let go? There isn't a formula to letting go, but there is, however, a way of thinking, perception if you will, that one must take on in order to let go successfully.

This mindset starts with accepting that God's ways are higher than our ways according to Isaiah 55:9. So let go of your ways and ideas as to how you feel God should manifest your desires. After you accept that God has His own way and time to make manifest our desires, the last step is to allow. Allow God to manifest your desires through whatever source He chooses, and to deliver it in the time He sees fit. God is unconventional. You must give Him creative freedom to move and operate if you want to manifest. This means, the process may not be the way you would have gone about it or the source may not fit the idea you had in mind. God does things for His glory, not ours!

The Holy Spirit gave me an awesome revelation surrounding letting go, and I must say, I was convicted to say the least. This revelation speaks to anyone who has something of value that they treasure. This could be a child, money or a pet. Let's look at all 3, shall we. As parents we typically drop our children off at a day care or leave them with a babysitter. We then proceed to go to work, run errands or whatever we had planned for that day. Never once do we drop them off with fear and anxiety. We're not calling the daycare or sitter every 5 minutes wondering if our child is okay. We simply drop them off confidently knowing that they are going to be well taken care of and will be there upon our return. The same goes for pet owners. You don't drop your pet off at doggy daycare or with the pet sitter fearing what will happen after you leave. Absolutely not! You go on vacation; you sip on your piña coladas on the beach of the Bahamas without one thought of fear or anxiety concerning your precious pet. How about those of you with no children or pets? But you entrust crooked banking institutions with your salaried checks, your bread and water. So much so, that you sign up for direct deposit. You make that deposit confidently knowing that your money will be there when time comes for you to withdraw it. Congratulations! You know how to detach. It is this same mindset, this level of confidence that we should operate in when detaching from our desires, petitions or prayers. We should "drop them off" knowing that all is well.

So tell me, how is it that you can trust daycares and sitters with your most precious gift and institutions that are synonymous with theft, yet we hesitate to let go of our desires and entrust God with them? These daycares/sitters and institutions don't have the power to give you the desires of your heart, yet God promises he'll give you your desires if you trust Him. God cares more about your hearts desire than your daycare/sitter and institutions, yet we treat Him like the thief. It's almost as if we fear if we let go, He's going to steal our desires and nothing will be made manifest. It's this kind of thinking that hinders our faith. How can we expect God to give us the desires of our heart, when we won't let go of them long enough for Him to fulfill them? This is why He states it's impossible to please Him without faith. Our lack of faith crosses over as an insult to the Creator of all things.

A lot of you "believers" look down on nonbelievers for not believing in God, yet you're one of them. Your lack of faith is the same as a person who doesn't believe in God. Faith is an action word. So you may argue that you do have faith, I would say you're right, but it's in something or someone other than God! Redirect your faith away from people, institutions and cultures and onto the God source and you'll manifest your desires easily and effortlessly!

DON'T GIVE UP

"And let us not be weary in well doing: for in due season we
shall reap, if we faint not"
-Galatians 6:9

I cannot stress this enough...DON'T GIVE UP!!! It is imperative that you exercise patience while you are manifesting a blessing. So many people abort the blessing because they lose heart during the waiting season. Everything has its season to come into fruition. A mother understands that it takes a baby 9 months before it can be born. A farmer understands that after his seed goes into the ground he must wait for harvest time before he can reap.

So why after a few weeks or months do you give up in frustration on your vision or dream? Don't you realize that even our visions and dreams have a gestation period? So after you visualize, speak (decree), and feel your vision into existence, allow it time to come to you. Its already been created it...now wait patiently and with a grateful heart. Grab your SWORD, DECREE and DECLARE your hopes into the atmosphere, VISUALIZE it coming to you and walk in your DOMINION!

Father God,

I thank you for every soul that purchased and read this book! I pray the Blessing of God over each and every one. Father, meet the needs of those that have read and is reading this book. Make their desires manifest in a way that will glorify you in the earth, in Jesus name,

~Amen

Made in the USA
Middletown, DE
03 May 2020